The *Me* I Sleep With

Embracing Rejection Without Empowering It

By:

Aasir Rayne

When I die, I would like for it to be known and said that I loved God, I loved people, and I lived to serve both. It is my heart to simply to please God in all that I am and all that I do. I desire that my life ever be proof that defeat is not an option because victory [through Jesus] always is.

I would like to take a moment and thank you for your support of this project. I am humbled that God provided this opportunity to touch your life in an intimate and tangible way. I pray that, as you read each entry in this book, you are challenged to evaluate your life and the matters of your heart and mind, and to make whatever changes necessary to live an abundantly prosperous life.

To each of you holding this book in your hands, viewing these words with your eyes, and hiding these truths in your hearts, may God establish and increase you.

I endeavor to challenge perspective, provoke change, encourage growth, attack dysfunction, and motivate a lifestyle of greatness.

Don't not let defeat, as a result of rejection, be your song. Write a new melody, within your heart, of love, security, and victory.

God Bless.

3 John 1:2-*Dear friend, I pray that you may prosper in every way, and be in good health physically, just as you are spiritually.*

Table of Contents

Introduction

"Being different, being unique is undeniably a fundamental characteristic of being human." ~Unknown

In this life, we will face some things that may cause us to question our reason for being. Though there are different factors in existence, as to why we wonder whether we are a mistake, there is one factor that reigns supreme...our little friend, Rejection. Rejection, an essential factor to the human dynamic, is outspoken and insensitive. Rejection is verbally and physically abusive, frequently attacking our emotions, our mind, and our bodies. Rejection refuses to be cast away or forgotten. If it can make us sigh, that will make it smile. If it can make us cry, that will make it laugh. Rejection can cause us to question why we were even born and can even go as far as to encourage us to want to die.

When we sleep, it wakes us...that's if it ever lets us go to sleep. We find it difficult to function with rejection, but we can't function without it either. Rejection's presence is inevitable; its impact is undeniable. We often let it direct our day, determine our worth, and dictate our relationships. We hope to conquer it, but fail, in every attempt. We have this innate desire to be needed, loved,

and accepted; rejection lurks around every corner, it seems, to ensure that we feel quite the opposite. Rejection is the quiet whisper that creates so many storms in our lives.

I have good news and bad news about rejection. Bad news---you cannot outlive it. Good news---you can outgrow the defeat you feel from it. There is a way to deal with rejection and all its proclivities. Even better, there is a way to function with rejection in our lives, without empowering it. "How?", you might ask. Good question. The answer---Embrace it. Yes, that is right. Embrace it.

Understand that when I say *embrace it,* I am, by no means, telling you to agree with what rejection makes you feel or think. When I say *embracc it,* I am speaking to the acceptance of its presence in your life, and the type of impact it can have when you agree to its truths. As we move forward in our conversation on walking out this life, successfully, even with rejection present, I would like to begin with a clear definition of rejection. To help better understand the purpose of our conversation, we will define rejection as *feeling as though one is missing out on or being denied something that matters, something that would, ultimately, determine and/or validate one's worth.*

So, "Why did he choose that title for this book?", you might be wondering? I mean, that title could have fit a few other topics, right? Well, the first reason I chose it is that I like the title; it really grabs your attention, and I have been waiting for quite some time to use it. The second reason is that we each have a side of us, that "Me", that no one sees or really knows about. It is the side of us that plays tug-a-war within to determine what works and what does not. I have discovered that, quite often, that hidden part of us is controlled by rejection, in all its many facets. As rejection is our biggest fear, it has the most control over our lives, in so many ways. And, if we do not build a healthy response to it, we will permit it to overtake and control us.

Now that we have established the meaning and we have an idea of how rejection attempts to position itself in our lives, let us discuss how we are to embrace, and not empower it. I encourage, as we continue our conversation, that you not just read, but evaluate. Even if you are one who feels you know yourself, and are sure about your worth, let this serve as a moment to reassess your level of assurance.

Purposed

by

Design

You Are Not an Accident

As we began, I want to be sure that, moving through this discussion, we hide these truths in our hearts, allow them to circulate through our minds, and speak them from our mouths. With that being said, announce this with me, "I am not an accident." Say it again, and slowly this time. "I am not an accident." Now, affirm this with me. "My existence is not a mistake. I am supposed to be here. And, I have something to offer."

It could be that when you were saying those things to yourself, for yourself, you did not really believe or take those words in. Maybe you have said similar before, so it really did not mean much. If that is the case, I encourage you to take a moment and repeat those declarations, once more, as you inhale and exhale. Our words have power; therefore, nothing we ever say, no matter how simple we consider it to be, is without effect. So, I encourage you to be intentional about what you declare and when you declare it.

Please understand that you are not an accident. Those are not just words; that is truth. I do not care how you came to be, there is nothing about who you are that is accidental. You were designed on purpose, with purpose. Can you believe that? Do you believe that?

Let's declare it. "I was designed on purpose, with purpose." Breathe that in. Ooh, that feels good to know. There are so many things in this life that we walk through that seem to contradict such a truth. Be it family dynamic, relationships, careers, religion, politics, disappointment, fear, loneliness, or the greatest impactor, rejection, we must continuously remind ourselves that *our very existence is intentional.* God's thought and design for you is so strategic, that you could not out-plan your destiny, your purpose, your worth, if you tried.

The greatest crisis to have ever existed in the world is that of *identity.* The most wide-spread epidemic is the fear of rejection. When you read the Christian bible, specifically in the book of Genesis, you find the first introduction of such fear being challenged. The serpent, oh so cunning, attacks Eve's fear of rejection, or rather her desire to be accepted. The whole point of the conversation was to get Eve to feel that she was being left out of something, and thus lacking worth. It worked. Like each of us has done, at some point in our lives, Eve's response to feeling rejected led her to doing something foolish and wrong, sabotaging her present and her future. The goal was to get Eve to feel as though she was not enough, and that because of it, God was holding out on her. It worked. She allowed the deception of rejection to empower insecurity within her, and her response changed her whole life, and the lives of those connected to her.

I have discovered that it is not so much about us not wanting to be rejected as it is about us not wanting to *feel* rejected. In all honesty, we like being rebels; so, the idea of rejection is not as intense as we would think because we pursue it. It is the *feeling* of rejection that gets us. "You can dislike me all you want; just don't let me feel disliked.", is what we are really feeling and thinking, most times. Here is one way we know most everything is about a feeling. You can sit in your bedroom, alone all day; you are good and do not mind having no one around or anything to do. This remains true until you start to feel alone.

Once the impact of loneliness kicks in, your day is ruined---because it is all about the feeling, not necessarily about the experience. For many the feeling is the experience because we are so emotionally driven. And this is true in almost every arena of a person's life. Do not believe me, go to church, to a concert, out on a date, to a game; until you feel excited or inspired, changed or elevated, you are not moved by what's going on. You are just there. It does not become a moment until you are "living" in it. Because "living in the moment" is more about the experience than the opportunity, and the experience is more about the feeling you get because of the opportunity you took advantage of. We live in a hyper-emotional world, where more is dictated by how one feels rather than the truth that should govern. Hyper-emotionalism is dangerous because many do not know how to control or respond to their emotions, leaving them quite imbalanced in life. But that is another conversation for another day.

The enemy uses those things that will manifest an emotional response to rejection, within us, to trip us up. "What is his biggest tool?", you might be wondering. That is an easy one---people. Now because we are made in the likeness and image of God, we have the innate desire to be needed, loved, and accepted. Some look for one more than the other (and that is usually based on position in the family). We were created to need God because He is all that we need, and desires to be so in our lives. We were created to seek love from God because His love is unconditional and without measure; it fills us. We are to seek acceptance from God because, as our Creator, He accepts us. Thus, God loves us, accepts us, and wants us to need Him completely.

So, let's be clear. There is nothing wrong with wanting to be any of those three things. However, we are supposed to be looking to God to manifest the fulfillment of those in our lives. We are to look to Him to need, love, and accept us; therefore, all other avenues are bonus. The problem comes when we look to any and everything else, especially people, to fill those spaces, attempting to validate our lives. You know, the whole notion of someone else "completing" us.

I would be remised, if I did not take a moment inform you that no one else can complete you. Let me repeat that once again. No one else can complete you. Even you are not able to love and accept yourself into completion. This searching for acceptance and approval introduces the concept and vice we call "Approval Addiction". Approval Addiction is just what it says, being addicted to the approval and acceptance of others to validate one's worth.

"Approval Addiction" is a prison with chains that only serves to choke out the freedom to be who God created you to be. It keeps you going in circles and cycles. It makes you an insecure *chameleon.* And it is detrimental to one's health and well-being. Understand that the acceptance you need comes from God. The rest is bonus. The only reason we should be concerned about what others think about us is as it regards honoring them. We should never give anyone the power to dictate our formation or the authority to change or rather dishonor our design.

So, how do you progress beyond "Approval Addiction"? First, by understanding that you are not an accident, and that you matter. Second, by rejecting the lie that you are a mistake. Now, maybe no one has ever told you that you matter or, when a person did, nothing was done to validate that he or she really meant it. So, let me say it to you and for you now.

You matter. You are important, and you have something wonderful to share with the world----You. God has created you with intention, with might, with validity, with worth. He has endowed you with greatness, with vision, with authority. And there is, absolutely, nothing you could ever be or do to change that.

You may have been born premature, which led to complications or physical ailments that you must contend with daily. You may be one who has difficulty learning or holding on to information. You may be one who is physically disproportionate. Maybe, from a young age, someone always told you or made you feel like something was wrong with you, and you felt like an outcast. Maybe your parents gave you up for adoption. Maybe your parents planned to abort you, and changed their minds, but every day they still treat you like a burden. I could go on and on with things that we deal with that make us feel like we are a mistake; there are so many. At the end of the day, the truth of the matter is that, regardless of what category you fall into, you are here because you belong here. And there is nothing on Earth that can change that.

I will end with this little nugget. So often, we get caught up in where we are rather than focusing on why we are. It causes us to miss moments of growth, moments of wisdom, moments of interaction, even moments of opportunity. As well, because we are not often where we want to be, we grow the habit of grumbling and complaining. We cannot be content because of the lens we are looking through, especially when we compare our *green grass* to someone else's.

I said all that to say this. **Do not confuse placement with positioning.** God is all about positioning. Many times, we may be placed in a particular environment, maybe even one we do not favor. However, everything about why we are there matters. We were positioned there to grow and to share.

Proverbs 3:5-6, an incredibly famous scripture amongst the Christian faith, exhorts us to "lean not to your own understanding, but in all of your ways, acknowledge Him (God), and He shall direct your path." I believe that our responsibility is not to set our path or order our steps. Our responsibility is to be submissive and obedient to the steps that God orders for us and walk them out. I believe that when we do that, everywhere we place our feet has impact because we are being positioned in that moment.

So, look through the lens of *positioning*, not the lens of *placement*. Placement will tell you that you have nothing to offer and, possibly, nothing to receive. Positioning will tell you that with little or much, it is still something; so, grow it and share it. Where you are, is not an accident.

It can grow you, if you let it. Who you are is not an accident. You have something to offer.

You Are Not Your Gifts

Now, I must throw this in here because it is extremely important for you to understand. **You are not your gifts.** I repeat. You are not your gifts. When you hit the Earth, God endowed you with the tools and resources needed to fulfill your assignment. You have been gifted to ensure that you have what you need to get the job done and walk out this life successfully. Remember, we spoke earlier about you being designed on purpose, with purpose.

When you make your gifts your identity, two things are liable to happen: 1) You change personas to fit the gift required in that moment. 2) When your gift is rejected, you internalize it as you are being rejected. You should never change to fit your gifts. As well, you should be adjusting to, not conforming to, your environments. When you internalize everything, you run the risk of limiting movement and growth because you are making it about you.

God has placed in each and every individual that has ever and will ever walk this Earth, a uniqueness. He has gifted each of us with what is needed to fulfill the purpose for which we were created. Though we may share gifts and talents, each of us have been equipped with what is specific to our purpose. So often, we allow people to intimidate us and demean what God has designed for our lives. We do not see the value in our gifts, usually because we are comparing them to the gifts of another. A question was asked to me recently, "If you found a belt that worked better, would you wear it?" My response was "No, not if mine's works fine." Because *it is all about what you perceive as better.* We must get away from comparison because it leads to complacency, ungratefulness, negative perspective, taking what is good and devaluing it because you think you found better.

In this case, the individual asking the question was equating the look of the belt with the quality of the belt. *Just because something may look nicer or better, does not mean that it is.* What was even more concerning, was that there was nothing wrong with the original belt; it simply had more history. The "better" belt was just a newer belt. Comparison is not your friend. When we compare gifts or abilities, we diminish our capacity to grow and to move our own essence in the best way, across the Earth.

Every single person on this planet has been gifted with talents, creativity, ideas, and even vision. Some are thinkers. Some are better with their hands. Some are more, publicly, influential. And others are better behind the scenes. I do, also recognize that there are those who have so many gifts and talents that they take little value in the ones that do not seem to be celebrated or spotlighted, socially, as much as some of their other gifts.

Sadly, there are even those who never embrace and appreciate the gifts God has given them, again, mainly because they are comparing their abilities to another's. In this, the fear of rejection dictates a great deal of their decisions and movements. How sad is it that we reject and deny our own awesomeness, comparing it to someone else's? We should be seeking for ourselves, "What is my niche?" "How do I take what's in me and work it in excellence, authentically?" *Seek it. Find it. Celebrate it. And utilize it.* Many of us never figure out what works for us because we spend too much time and energy mimicking.

God never calls us to something without giving us what we need to make it happen. The gifts are simply the things that introduce another level of God's glory into the Earth and equip you with what you need to move in the Earth, effectively. If one's gift determined his or her identity, everyone would be everything, all the time. Everybody sings. Does that make everyone singers? Everyone dances, does that make everyone dancers? I believe we have a few television-based, talent shows that can prove gifts do not make the person (i.e.-American Idol, So You Think You Can Dance, Cupcake Wars, Top Chef).

We see so many times, especially through media and sports, the vice of individuals making their gifts their identity. Parents, teachers, mentors and authority figures from all walks of life, even peers tell us that we are the gift we operate in. This is one reason why so many people never discover who they really are, or the full capacity of what they can accomplish. This is rough because we live out the lowest potential of ourselves, in many cases, all due to lack of self-awareness. Rejection tells us that we must keep changing to fit what we are doing. Thus, we conform to our abilities. Even worse, we have been conditioned to be insecure about our gifts, and our insecurities have elevated our level of selfishness. And every time the presentation of our gift is rejected, those insecurities are validated and nurtured [by rejection].

That is why most people do not do what they love. They seek out careers that will win the approval of others or make them feel like they finally have what it takes. They are so focused on what is expected of them, what will get them spotlighted, what will get them praised. This should not be the goal. So, say this with me, "I am not my gifts." "My gifts don't make me. They enable me." Now inhale and exhale. Take that in. Remember, words have power. What you say, you think. And what you think, you say.

You Are Not for Sale

We base our level of worth, as well as our level of success or failure, on how people perceive and respond to what we say and do. That is how businesses function. It should not be how people function. You are not trying to sell yourself. You are trying to introduce yourself. And just like with a company that introduces a product to the public, just because you introduce yourself does not mean that you will be, initially, liked and accepted. It does not mean that you will be accepted at all.

How sad is it for us to be willing to settle for being accepted, even if we are not liked? I refuse to walk around life being okay with just being tolerated. I have too much to offer to just be tolerated. And so do you. Say this with me, "I, [*Insert your name*], refuse to settle for just being tolerated. I have too much to offer to just be tolerated." Tuck that in your soul somewhere. You have too much to offer to settle for just being.

Everyone knows that supply is all about demand. If there is no demand, there will be no supply. Thus, companies respond to the demand of the consumers. They market and advertise based on the needs and desires of the audience. They brand based on the perception or potential of the consumer. And though a company may have a standard brand or a signature by which you can recognize it, some flexibility and conforming is necessary for progression. Certain companies even go to the extent of, continuously, conforming to the ever-changing desires of the consumer to stay relevant. This is not always a healthy thing and some companies do not last because of the back and forth that occurs trying to meet demand.

Ironically, we are the same way. We try to sell ourselves to others. We conform to the preferences and perceptions of others. We change standards, beliefs, appearances, and behavior, all to fit the image and mold projected onto us, the demand of others, and what we believe is expected of us. We become insecure *chameleons*, not just adapting to whatever environment we are in, but changing to fit said environment. All this, to get folks to like us. We were created too uniquely to mimic or be a *social chameleon.*

That is such a horrible way to live---never really knowing who you are, allowing others to dictate who you will become. By doing so, you are living out the very epitome of Multiple Personality Disorder, without the clinical diagnosis. Supply and Demand was never meant to become the basis for which we determine human value. Stop, I repeat, stop trying to sell yourself to the highest bidder. You will keep trying to sell yourself only to later end up on "Clearance". You keep trying to be purchased by people who cannot afford you. Yet, the one who can, put Himself on display in your place, so you would not have to keep marketing yourself.

You are officially unmarketable, and that is not a bad thing. It means that no one can put a price on you. The price Jesus paid has made you unaffordable. You are, by definition, priceless. And catch this. No one has ever been able to outbuy Him or outbid Him.

So, repeat after me, and say this within yourself, not just at yourself. "I am not for sale." "I am priceless and therefore, cannot be bought." "I am a gift and a treasure, not a product on a shelf." Soak that in. "I am not a product on a shelf. I am a gift and a treasure." That is what I call a "rainy day" confession. When you feel unappreciated or taken advantage of, when you feel used and abused, when you feel rejected and neglected, when you feel like you are just existing in a space, when you feel like the butt of everyone's jokes, when you are in a relationship where you are not growing, when your life tells you that you have nothing to offer and that you are wasting your time, when you feel any of these things, that is the announcement you have to speak into yourself. Let it echo in your soul.

Now, I want you to take a moment and think about the shirt that says, "This is what AWESOME looks like." I am sure you have seen someone wearing it, or on a shelf at Wal-Mart. If you do not have one, you should purchase one because it is a true statement that you are choosing to, publicly, acknowledge. You are awesome. You are awesome because God says you are awesome. No other reason is needed. There is nothing you must do to make it so.

This is being extra, I know, but it will also be a little comical; wear the shirt, and every time it catches someone's eye, or someone ask where you got it, be sure to look at them and say, "You're welcomed." Just kidding. You do not have to say it, but you should, definitely, think it. And thinking or saying it does not mean you are arrogant; such a statement is saying that you recognize that you are a wonderful work of art, hand-crafted by God, that someone else has the privilege of being introduced to, and you agree with that truth.

Back to the point. If we are all awesome and priceless, why do we keep trying to compare ourselves to other priceless masterpieces? If we are all priceless, no one's value can surpass another's, right? Rejection and comparison, apparently, think differently. They teach us to never, ever, consider ourselves worthy, and to never consider ourselves loved, needed, or accepted. They teach us that there is always going to be something missing, something lacking, something broken in our lives. We are supposed to be the light in a dark place, but with the relationship we have with rejection, you would think that the Grim Reaper is our shadow. And man, does he do damage to our light. He makes us feel so inadequate. We do so much to move beyond the lack of worth we feel, and, quite often, it only hurts us more. Your worth cannot be discounted. You are priceless, remember? Whatever you do in life, do not ever exchange quality for quantitative favor from men and women who will live on after you die. So, say this with me again, "I am not for sale."

You Are Not Unlovable

The biggest lie that you will ever hear is that you are not worthy of love. So, let us settle this right now. **There is nowhere that you can go, in this life, and *love* not be available to you.** Crazy to start off my first sentence so *boldly*, huh? It does not matter what form *love* is manifested in, you will always have a *tangible* expression of love accessible to you, dare I say, forced upon you. Therefore, **you can never be unlovable.** You can be intolerable (by others). You can even be rejected (also by others). But **you will never, ever be unlovable.** There is, absolutely, nothing you can do to make you worthy or unworthy of love, no matter how amazing or messed up you may consider yourself.

I know, I know "God, thank You for loving me, even when I was unlovable." sounds cute to say when we talk about God's unconditional love for us. *But it is this kind of love (unconditional) that makes it impossible not to be loved.* How love is gifted to you or received from you has nothing to do with the truth that love will always be present in your life. God is love. Love is a life source. Therefore, if love is the very air you breathe, how can you ever be without it?

You may be one who has heard me say this before; if so, I want to reiterate it. If this is new to you, pay close attention. *You make the Gospel relevant. Jesus died for you.* And yes, I know that things in life seem to contradict such truth. Be it family members, physical ailments, various disappointments incurred through life's journey, environment, insecurities, etc., you will always find something that will work to make you believe that no one, not even God (the very epitome of love) could value you so much. I am here to tell you that *your worth is not based on what you say and do.* What you say and do is based on how much of your worth you recognize and appreciate. You will always possess an *immeasurable* amount of worth.

I do not care how you may categorize yourself. Be it nice and fine or ugly and unkind. Be it heterosexual or homosexual, transgender or transsexual. Be it too short or too tall, too skinny or too fat. Be it you feel youthful and vibrant or old and tired, like a treasure or like trash,...and the list goes on and on. It does not matter...GOD LOVES YOU. That is an unescapable truth in your life. Even when we do things to dishonor Him, His love never changes for us.

It does not matter how many times you feel that you have failed---God loves you. It does not even matter how many times you feel you have succeeded---God loves you. It does not matter how many people told you that you would never be anything or add up to much---God loves you. It does not matter if everyone held you to a high standard and not only expected but required a level of success you have never been able to meet---God loves you. It does not matter if you were abandoned at birth or triumphant over an abortion---God loves you. It does not matter if you were adopted or the youngest of 12 children---God loves you. Man, oh man, could this list go on forever. The point is that it does not matter what *lies* life has presented and will present you, in this moment and those to follow, you are not allowed to believe the *lie* that you do not matter, and you are not loved.

You will never, ever, be unlovable. You will never, ever, be without value. You will never, ever, be without divine purpose. You will never, ever, be invisible, or irrelevant. And listen, people are not God. *God is ever-mindful of you even when you are not mindful of Him.* He continues to love you even when you do not recognize it, or when people work to blind you from it. I will say it again. **Your worth is immeasurable.** Think about it.

You are a one-of-a-kind, fine design. There is, absolutely, no one on this Earth quite like you.

Let's take a look at something, briefly. In reading the Bible, you will find in Matthew 26, Mark 14, and Luke 7, a recounting of a woman breaking open an alabaster box to pour out the contents upon Jesus. We always love talking about the value placed on the perfume that she broke over and poured out on Jesus. We speak to how priceless that oil was. You hear about how those sitting in the room were discussing how much money the perfume cost, how much she could have made if she sold it, and how foolish she was to do such a thing. However, one of the wonderful things I appreciate about this account is that the woman took all value off the perfume when she recognized the value of Jesus, Himself. She placed so much stock in Jesus and His worth (being priceless) that the perfume she poured then became just as priceless, and everything she had to contribute to Him became priceless.

Simply put, perfume/cologne does not have value until it hits your skin. It was the breaking open that highlighted that the oil had value; it was the vessel it was placed on that signified and determined how much [value it possessed]. We make it seem like breaking the box and perfume being opened was such a sacrifice because we highlight the worth of the perfume. We fail to realize that the vessel it was showered upon, ultimately, determined the value of the perfume...not the other way around. It became a matter of "What do I have to offer you that can express to you, properly, my recognition of and appreciation for who you are?"

And it is the same thing when it comes to people. If I have a child, my child is not priceless because it is my seed. It is priceless because it is His (God's) seed, gifted to me. I recognize that the child is a one-of-a-kind, immeasurable gift to my life, and to the Earth. And just like the perfume became priceless because the woman with the alabaster box recognized that who she was offering it to was priceless, so does God with you.

God never fails to give us His best. And His love is without condition; all He ask is that we accept it. We put in way too much energy trying to find someone or even something to love us. We invest way too much in trying to get others to give us a proper appraisal. Listen you, yes you...whichever "you" is reading this, read me, and read me well: **You are the one thing that money cannot buy.**

And for the one who is or has been a victim of sex trafficking, prostitution, slavery, etc., you may say that this is disputable. I am telling you that there is no measure of money or pleasure that could ever truly accompany the level of worth you, as the workmanship of the hand of God, possess.

And, because God is the only one who can determine your worth, it goes without saying (but I am going to say it again anyway) **you are priceless.** Do not believe me, read John 3:16 (for starters...there are plenty more scriptures to support my claim). You have heard it said before, "Love yourself." Well, I am here to tell you that you cannot. One reason is because you are so invaluable to that you do not have the capacity to, holistically, appreciate the masterpiece you are. You can, however, embrace the love that God has to offer you, through the many facets of it that He has made, readily, available to you, in every stage of your life. Be careful not to make those things idols though.

God loves and values you way too much to allow you to walk through life without being able to touch Him (love) at every turn. I have heard so many people say that they cannot hear God or that they don't believe in God, or even ask "What does He look like and how to find Him?" My response is this: If you have ever known love, and I mean true love (not these shallow, self-centered, humanized versions of love), if you have ever known even an ounce of love, you have encountered God. The breath you breathe is love, regardless of how you use it (honorably or wickedly); you cannot function without. Which would lead one (that *one* being me, of course) to say that you cannot function without God (another topic for another day).

You could be orphaned, homeless, a victim of abuse, bullied, insecure, an addict, physically impaired, mentally impaired, it does not matter. I do not care what experiences you have and will have, there will always be a form of love available and eager to attach itself to your life, to hold you up and move you. There will always be something gifted to you that can help grow hope, love, confidence, and security in you. Do not miss those moments looking for something that is not there (and not worth it). Also, don't be afraid to give one moment up because you will have an opportunity to grab ahold to an even better one.

I will conclude with this. I was once asked, "How did you come to trust the love of God?" My answer was: "Throughout my life, I have experienced a number of things that only the love of God could walk me through, cover me in, protect me from, lift me above, and push me beyond. It has been the only constant, unrelenting, irresistible, undeniable guiding force in my life." **It is, absolutely, impossible for you to be unlovable.**

Love in its purest form is sacrificial. God has shown that there is no amount of sacrifice to great that He would not give to prove how much He loves you. So, whenever you see it, hear it, feel it, or taste it, be sure to appreciate it, and then share it. And if you, currently, have a difficult time believing that you are loved, I welcome you to know and believe this: God loves you and I do too. "Don't believe me? Just watch!"

What

Lies

Beneath

You Are Not What They Call You

Be careful about who you let have a voice in your life. Others will always have something to say. The voices we choose to entertain matter. What we give ear to, inwardly and outwardly, matters. From the time we are conceived, we have people speaking over us and into us. We cannot always help what they have to say, or even when they will say it. However, we can control how much of it we choose to agree with. There are times when we can decide who we allow to speak into our lives, but whether we can or cannot, we should always be careful who we lend our ears to.

Now, this is not always people close to us or in our corner. There are many times that we adhere to the perception of people who do not even know us. We let people talk, and we tune in and match their frequencies. Listen!---Stop listening so hard. Most of the time we listen due to insecurity of being left out. We just have to know. No, you do not have to know. We, so often, thirst to know what others think about us. Many times, what they have to say has little to no relevance to the wellness of our souls. We seek validation and security in other insecure individuals. Validation should not come from other people. True validation is an inward security that can only exist when you agree with what God has to say about who we are. Anyone can deny, but no one can change how God feels about you, the workmanship of His hand.

Sometimes, we set ourselves up. We do everything possible to be involved, so we do not feel rejected, only to end up being rejected anyway. I would much rather you say nothing to me, than say something that is going to destroy me and go against the truth of my being. We listen for falsities, and then get mad at those who speak them. And this is because, deep down, we agree. When we entertain what people have to say about us and then hide those things in our heart and mind, we empower both the words and the people. Words have power and people have relevance. Thus, we must be cautious of how much we empower the words and the presence of others in our lives.

So, be careful of how much of what others have to say about you and your life that you chose to entertain and agree with. And another thing---Keep people out of your business! Stop telling people your business. Not everyone can handle your stuff. And not everyone needs to have access to your life like that. That is really about seeking attention and approval; it benefits you very little. In addition, stop seeking advice from people who do not empathize with you or have wisdom. As well, look for walkers, not talkers. Stop letting people, who do not know who they are, tell you who you are supposed to be. The world is full of broken people trying to fix and direct other broken people. Most relationships are this way. Stop letting insecure people tell you how to live securely.

We have this thing we do where we look to people to tell us who we are. In doing so, we empower them to mold and shape us into their vision. We answer to the names they call us and the assignments they give us. The problem is when, answering to the call of man or the name man gives us, we neglect to answer to the name God gave us and His call. There is no one on Earth who can tell you who you are like God can.

Every human being speaks from his or her point of reference. We build people up and tear people down based on our point of view, our basic beliefs, and our inner securities (or lack thereof). See...I am doing it now. If the point of reference is tainted, the affirmation will be also. Most lack proper perspective, and therefore, project that corrupt view onto others. Strangely enough, rejection plays a major role in the way we form our views of life, of people, of God, of self. I have learned that there are way too many people living from a perspective created from rejection and comparison rather than from truth and love.

If you are a young man who has had a poor representation of manhood from your father or other male figures, do not believe the lie, that you have been told, that you will be or you are "just like your daddy". You possess the ability to outgrow that. If you are a young lady, whose mother has had numerous kids from different fathers, and is struggling to take care of each of them, do not believe the lie that such a life also belongs to you. If you were told that you will not be anything without a college degree, but some dude flipping burgers for little to nothing, do not believe that lie. If you were told that playing sports is your only avenue to success, do not believe that lie. We could go on and on with a list of things we are told, over the course of our lives, that we nurture into truths. Sadly, we fear rejection, whether we live them out or not. That is just too much pressure.

Stop for a minute, and ask this profoundly important question, "God, what is the story you wrote about me?" Now I want you to take a moment (and it may be more than a moment---it could be a week) and think of all the things you have been told you were and would be, as well as all the things you have been told were not and could not be. Think very deeply. Again, you may be doing this for a few days. Do you have some things in mind? If so, say this with me. "I am more than what they say. I am more than what they see. I am more than what I hear. I am more than who I am told I am. I am more than who I am told to be." There is something extraordinary about you and within you. You must believe that, regardless of any outside stimuli.

Listen. The two greatest discoveries you will ever have in this world are 1) a discovery of who God is and 2) a discovery of who you are [in Him]. We are made in God's likeness and image. Therefore, the more you discover about Him, the more you discover about you. With that discovery, you can conclude that you are extraordinary, beyond measure. With that discovery, you are able to decide not to settle for being anything less than the best, most authentic rendition of yourself.

Now, I must take a moment to apologize on behalf of those who have been a part of the history of poorly representing God in His goodness and love, specifically those of the Christian faith. Many of us have do not a detrimental job of being a proper representation of what it looks like to walk in truth and love. And, I know, with the way the world and people are, it may be difficult for you to read some of this. Maybe you do not believe in, do not trust, don't understand, or you may even be angry at God. I hope that you can see beyond that to the point of the message. And, maybe, just maybe, you will find the truth of God love in it too. Because, ultimately, there is no rejection in Him.

The problem many of us have, and why we settle for "likes" rather than honor, is that we are not self-aware. So many, walk through life blind because we allow our insecurities to be our vision and our point of reference. Even worse, very few take time to have conversations with ourselves about who we are. I am always amazed and sadden at the number of individuals, particularly adults, that I encounter that live so insecurely because they have not settled in their identity and worth. So many lack awareness of self, and thus, have not the ability to own the glorious truth of their invaluable worth. This is what I know---It is imperative that I have conversations with the "Me" I sleep with. I consider him like a watch; I need to know how he ticks. We must see the importance in knowing the *mechanics* of our soul. As much as you must learn why you work, it is just as important (if not more so) for you to learn how you work.

Many of us do not know who we are, so we settle for allowing others to tell us. I have found that the most loving individuals in my life, can and will fail to empower me with the truth of who I am. The only reliable source for that is the One who created me, God. I believe God tells us who we are, and people reap the benefit when we walk that thing out. And yes, I believe God uses others to help in that discovery; however, we should never seek identity or security in how another views us.

We keep letting people who do not know who they are tell us who we are. And, even worse, we stop asking God. Do not stop asking. I am going to throw this little "Life nugget" in here...for free, of course. *If you stop asking, you stop learning. And, if you stop learning, you stop growing.* So, let us ask this question again, together. "God, what is the story you wrote about me, when you thought me up?"

This is what I need you to understand. You are not who they call you. I repeat, you are not who they call you. You are who God calls you to be. Anything outside of who God says you are and what He says you can do, is a lie. Know this. Again, you may not even believe in the God I believe in. I must believe that there is a God who wants a far better life for us than we have ability to imagine, no matter how impossible it may seem.

Consider yourself a fruit-bearing tree. Each time you grab ahold to and claim the rejection directed at you or perceived by you from another, you empower that person to climb up and snatch good fruit from the very heart of your tree.

There are many things that scratch the surface of a person's being. There are few things that can touch the essence of a person. Rejection is one of those few things. What are you letting grab at your heart, and why? And what are you answering to? Take time to think about it and address it, so that you can obtain healing and freedom...And grow even better fruit, in your life.

You Are Not the Lies You Believe About Yourself

Stop attaching yourself to the names you are called, the titles you are given, the gifts you have. Those things are no more than you allow them to be. If what someone, inclusive of yourself, is saying is contrary to what God says about you, it is dead, and it is killing you. Stop empowering dead things. *If it does not increase you, it decreases you.* We spend too much time trying to empower ourselves with things that do not empower us.

The big problem arises not just when we believe the lies spoken into us by others, but when we begin to live out those lies as truths. When we start to agree with what people think of us and live it out, life gets crazy. Am I right? Foolishly, we make the mistake of letting people's opinions become our truths, which can, in turn, become our prison. Now, I must say this, so that we do not misunderstand what I am trying to relay. *Not everything that someone says about you or sees in or for you is wrong. Not everything that we are told about ourselves is a lie. We must challenge everything with truth. Just because you do not like or want to believe what someone sees in you or says about you does not mean you get to make that out to be a lie. Truth is truth. Do not dismiss*

We internalize the lies and make them our own truths. This is especially true when situations in life seem to agree and validate. The rejection we feel, the neglect we feel, the disappointment we feel, they all seem to grow, in us, self-hate and discouragement, fear and anxiety, anger and resentment. You are not the lies you have begun to believe about yourself. To know what those lies are, you are going to have to take some time to self-evaluate.

I want to take a moment and share something with you because I know it to be truly relevant to not just this conversation, but our lives. I spoke, earlier about the importance of being self-aware. At a young age, we each have an experience that causes us to feel rejected. Throughout life, we have numerous experiences that seem to validate what we felt that first time, that initial feeling of rejection, loss, despair, fear, etc. Dangerously, we tuck away, in our subconscious, the initial experience, so that we do not have to deal with it or because we do not know how to. What we fell to realize is that just because a thing lies dormant within us does not mean that it is inactive within us. I have heard many times, "Oh, I let that go years ago." or "I forgot about that." If you did not take time to address it, and you just decided to push it off, you did not let it go. You stored it. And what is stored maintains presence and value, and can be used again, until it is *completely* discarded. Even worse, I have heard, "I don't know where it all started." I know it can be overwhelming, but if you do not know where rejection, fear, abandonment, despair, and any other issue began, you must honor yourself by taking time to dig deep and find out. Then address it. We may not always be reminded of the initial experience each time we feel rejected, but what we felt from that experience is validated every time something happens to promote the feeling of rejection. *You must address the root, or the tree will always be in jeopardy.*

So, various experiences produce various lies. Throughout our lives, we allow those lies to be validated and become a part of us. We are going to go through a few lies now and combat them. Say these with me. "I am not unlovable." "I am not a failure." "I am not worthless." "I am not ugly." "I am not a reject." "I am not a problem." Now, I understand that with every "I am not" there should also be an "I am". So, say these with me, and mean these when you say them. "I am lovable." "I am priceless. My worth is beyond measure." "I am beautiful." Guys, if you do not feel comfortable saying "beautiful" say "I am handsome." or "I look awesome." Let us keep it going. Now, really point to yourself on these, and soak them in. "I am accepted." "I am loved." "I am needed." "I matter. Yes, I matter." Does that feel good or what?!? And do not be embarrassed if you shed a few tears. That means you felt what you were saying.

Now, I do not want to be naïve enough to think that just because you said it, that you believe and agree with it. I know that, sometimes, we must create an echo of truth on the inside before it can truly be expressed outwardly. So, I encourage you to continue to recite and resound these truths in your heart and soul. Your heart knows truth when it hears it. Do not let your mind outtalk the truth that seeks to resonate in your soul. Lock it in your heart, recite it in your mind, continuously, then walk it out.

Be, oh so, careful not to take on the lies that others tell you about yourself, especially to the point of agreeing with them and living them out as your own personal truths. It is a horrible feeling when you validate another's truth(s) of you, when everything within you is telling you it is wrong. Remember to trust what is within you over what is around you. What's around you is ever-changing and unfaithful. What is within you knows truth and provides you with an opportunity to say "Yes" or "No" to living that truth out. Use what you see around you to teach you, as everything, everyone, every moment can be a lesson, if you let it. Do not allow rejection to mold your truth because, in doing so, you will eventually dismiss and deny truth for what is familiar, comfortable, and appropriate for the moment. Rejection will cause you to settle for the common regardless of how dysfunctional it may be. And rejection will have you living lies, as you deny the truth of who you are.

You Are Not Your Failures

We often get caught up in past failures. A common question, as a result, is "How do I forgive myself [for my past]?" You, first, must understand that you cannot forgive yourself. It is, humanly, impossible to love, much less forgive, one's self. Our hearts are too wicked. If we could forgive ourselves, Jesus would have never had to come. Our responsibility is to embrace the love, the forgiveness, the grace, the mercy, and all the other amenities God has made available to us, as we walk this Earth and grow in relationship with Him.

So, now that that is settled. One of the biggest "self" problems created from getting caught up in your past is that you begin to compare yourself to a "you" that does not exist. And this is two-fold. We tend to set expectations of who we should be, inclusive of what we should be doing. We often define success, as well as our worth, based on whether we meet those expectations. This is foolish and detrimental.

We get lost in those failures, just the same as when we have successes. Thus, as we take steps forward, we halt to compare our present (and even our future) state to the person that failed. We omit the realization that such an individual no longer exist anymore. Secondly, we set expectations for who we hope to be in our future. We compare our present and past state to that person, usually fearing that we cannot be who we see. We do not give ourselves any room to fail, which alleviates any opportunity for recovery. The rejection induced, because of failed expectations has the ability to entrap us within those expectations---the *shoulda, coulda, woulda's* of life.

Stop imprisoning yourself to who you were, where you were, who you could be, and where you could be. Those people do not exist. Your past is gone. Your future is not here. Who are you now, and what can you do to honor the breath that you breathe in this moment, should be the focus. This does not mean that you do not need a vision, but *if you take the vision of your past, allow it to dominate the vision of your present, and dictate the vision of your future, you will go nowhere, fast and hard.* So, since we are naturally going to consider our past, I will advise you to do so in this manner---Consider lessons learned for the purpose of wisdom and growth. At the point that rejection (most likely in the form of failed attempts or expectations not met) rears its ugly head, move on and move forward from that moment in the past, you are standing in.

One of the reasons focusing on our failures is such a problem is because the rejection we experienced would have us believe that we are our failures. This is a big thing for men because men invest so much thought, energy, research, accountability, even vulnerability into something, that they expect that it is going to work. So, men leave little to no room for fallout. Men are, naturally, fixers. What men cannot fix they consider a failure. And because men have been conditioned to the lie that failure is not an option, rejection has a "field day" when something does not go as planned. Men self-inflict and internalize. This is not a healthy way to respond to failure.

A man is taught to win at all cost, and he is a failure, if he does not. Therefore, the fear of rejection, due to a lack of accomplishment in an area, is one reason why men work themselves to death with production, but little passion, and no fulfillment. I believe we all have this problem in one way or another, male and female alike. We produce, but there is little to no passion or fulfillment involved. Life is our assembly line, and we are *worker-bees* just trying to survive and get the job done. This is such a poor way to live. But rejection acclaims that, if we do not do, we cannot be.

Understand this. You will fail at some things. Failure does not equate to defeat. I believe one of the reasons we are so scared to fail is because we believe the lie that failure is defeat. You are more likely to be defeated by not doing something than you are by doing it and failing at it. The fear of rejection encourages us not to even try.

So, say this with me because I want to help you get away from the vice of entrapping yourself in the *shoulda, coulda, woulda's* of life. "I am not my past." "I am not the failure I experienced." "I am what I believe, so I choose to believe the best." "I believe in my future. I refuse to dishonor my present." "I am not my bad decisions." "I am more than what I see." "I am more than what I do." "The life that has been granted to me is worth every failure I produce." "I am not defined by my successes. I am not defined by my failures. I am defined by my Creator, and the truth and love that I live out." That was a lot to say, right? I hope you took your time in saying it all. Even more so, I hope you meant every word. Do not let failure become your identity. Allow failure to be an opportunity. Failure is human. Defeat does not have to be. And, victory is inevitable, and tangible.

You Are Not the Lies You Choose to Wear

If you are familiar with the X-Men saga, you may know that Professor X, eventually, had a son named David, which we would later come to know as Legion. Now Legion, or David, as I prefer to call him in this text (I do not want anyone to get unnerved.), had numerous superpowers (a few of which I wish I had). Strangely enough, each of his superpowers were controlled by a different personality. He had multiple people inside of his head; depending on which was dominating his mind at the time, that would determine what power manifested itself. Basically, *whatever controlled him, inwardly, determined what he produced, outwardly.* Now, that will preach. There were a few personalities that were far more dominate and powerful than the others, and boy, did they drive David crazy, fighting each other for full control over his mind and body. Sadly, with all that was going on within him, he had little to no control over his own life, mind, actions, body, or emotions. He was, by all accounts, mentally ill and unstable. He hurt a few people, along the way, as a result. Even crazier than multiple personalities, David could steal or absorb another's mind and personality, and if they had powers, the powers that person possessed, as well. How can someone that powerful, be so unhinged?

Take a moment and think about your own life. In a sense, we are a lot like Legion. We invite tons of personalities into our lives and lose ourselves trying to live for and like others. It is sad how many things we have loved about life, about ourselves, even about other people that we allowed what others could or did say and do, and the rejection we felt or perceived, as a result, to cause us to change our minds and our hearts towards. What superpowers---gifts, talents, passions, visions have you allowed to change or die over the years, not because you grew, and life no longer required them, but because of the voices you entertained and the lack of acceptance you experienced or the rejection you assumed you would experience from others? How often have you tried to drain people of their essence, taking it as your own...because you did not know and/or did not solidify who you were? David's problem was that he could not be himself because he spent too much time being someone else. Do you have this same problem?

So often, we drain people trying to get them to prove to us that we matter. We drain people of their time and energy, of their very essence, trying to prove that we are loved, accepted, and needed. That is so selfish. Even worse, we take on the identities of the people we meet and grow with because we lack validity of self. It is one thing to adopt behaviors; it is another to adopt lifestyles and character.

I have heard it said many times that "Kids are so cruel." I only agree in part. Here is why. Children can be cruel, yes. I believe more than a child's ability to be cruel, children are driven, innately, by truth. Simply put, kids are honest. They have no filters. They say what they think based on what they see and what they feel.

Not having a filter means that regardless of whether what is said is kind or hurtful, a child feels compelled to speak his or her truth. I know you were told once or twice, as a child, "You don't have to say everything that comes to mind." or "Think before you speak." That is because, at such a young age, you do not think as much about filters and boundaries. You just think and speak your version of truth. I believe that we all start off with that level of honesty and do not pick-up filters until we are taught to wear masks. You have no filters until you are taught to wear masks, and a need for those filters arise, to maintain your masks. And yes, some filters are presented in the form of healthy boundaries; the problem with that comes when there is not healthy reasoning given to bring about an understanding of the need for such boundaries.

We compare the elderly and toddlers to each other regarding their honesty, because as a kid, you don't know filters, and as an older individual, you no longer see the need for them. Both have the mindset of *take me as I am* because, at those ages, they see no need to be anyone else. How wonderful would it be if we all could say that, respectfully, of course? We are far too concerned about what others think about us. What do you think about you, is the question?

Sadly, it is because, from an incredibly young age, we are conditioned to conform. We go from being told and even shown the possibilities, all the things we can do and can achieve, to being told what we should not do and what is not acceptable. From the way we think to the way we behave, from what we wear to what we say, we are taught to lay aside authenticity and individuality to *fit in*, to choose normal over extraordinary. We are conditioned to believe that, if we do not look and sound like everyone else, something is wrong with us, and we will be made an outcast. Thus, over the years, we grow into the role of *humanized chameleon.* We lose ourselves to *look the part.* And so, daily, we walk around exchanging masks based on the interaction, the environment, the need we are trying to meet, or the goal we are trying to achieve. Every single mask we put on is based on two things: the lack of self-awareness and the fear of rejection.

We want to be accepted so bad. You are asking someone to love your masks. They will love you when they see you. How ridiculous is it to get upset when people reject your masks? After all, you wanted them to accept the real you anyway, right? We were never called to mimic. And we were never meant to wear masks.

We understand that children mimic until they become. Unfortunately, we carry that same habit into adulthood. The problem is that such does not just reign true when it comes to hearing and seeing others, but also when we hear and see ourselves. Anything we are, continually, taught to say or do becomes a habit, and is then engraved into our minds. This means that as both a mirror and a reflection, we can reflect, inwardly, just as much as we do outwardly. This is a part of the process of internalization. It is also why some people seem to choose to remain a victim. They keep self-reflecting a damaged image, viewed through a cracked mirror.

Over the years, we like David, have had numerous personas fighting for domination and control over our lives. Sometimes, we have put up a fight, and other times, we have just let them have at it. Our fear of rejection has been a major factor in such decisions. And so, we keep making and wearing masks, hoping that one of them will get us love and acceptance. This was never God's desire towards our design. We have become *humanized chameleons* trying to fit in when we are called to stand out. *If I lose you and lose nothing, you have done a poor job of introducing me to the gift that you are.* There should be something about you that stands out to the rest of the world...and that something is you. Not what you say. Not what you do. But you, yourself should be what stands out. Masterpieces are original, authentic, and extraordinary in nature and by design. *Time out for settling for being an updated version of the outdated clone of an original masterpiece.* We are not cell

phones. Take the masks off. Throw them away. You
are not the lies you wear each day.

Stop

Begging!

You Don't Need to be Needed

One of the main reasons why we struggle with rejection is not because we want to be accepted, but because we want to be needed. *You cannot determine worth by need.* Remember, we talked about supply and demand earlier. Businesses can determine worth by need; you should not. Human needs change. Therefore, we should never lock our worth into whether someone needs us. The truth is that we will not always be needed. In trying to determine worth by need, we leave room for rejection to creep in and stir us. Knowing that you are needed and needing to be needed are two different things. The same is true in knowing that you matter and needing to matter.

Not being needed does not mean you do not matter. **You must give people permission not to need you.** If you obligate others to need you, you become inefficient when they do not. You must know that whatever space you are in, you are enough. When you stop obligating people to need you, you will not be lost and angry when they don't need you anymore. In fact, that will free you up from the frustration caused by many times in life that people do not even recognize you. Say this with me, "I am enough."

Being rejected does not make you any less valuable than being accepted makes you important. You were important and valuable when God created you. God's initial thought of you was so grand that He concluded "By any means necessary, the world needs to be introduced to this piece of Me." I believe that in our moment of conception was God saying, "The world is ready for you now.", and that our birth was God saying, "Let us get to work." There are those who ask, "How do you know God is real?" Well, you are that proof---that God is real and God is love.

Rejection is proof that people cannot validate us. God has never and will never reject us. In fact, all He has ever desired from us is relationship. We keep looking to people to love, accept, and need us, without condition. How? The very body they have comes with condition. For most, a person will honor another at the level to which he or she honors his or herself. That is the capacity to which that person has to reciprocate love and acceptance. We drain people of their essence trying to get them to not only need us, but to need us more than we need them or than they need God.

I believe it is because we want to be loved that we seek out being needed, and because we want to be needed that we seek out being accepted. Know this: **You are loved. You are needed. You are accepted.** And there is not one thing, to ever exist, that can change that. We love to be needed, so that we can be involved. We think that being involved means we are accepted. Wrong. And just because you may be needed, does not mean that you are necessary.

We are supposed to be needed so that we can make [positive] impact. One's involvement is not necessary outside of the impact made or lesson learned from his or her presence and behavior. Rejection is not the absence of need; it is the absence of want. It is okay for someone not to want you, just as much as it is for someone not to need you. Say this with me, "It is okay for me not to be needed." "I will not require anyone to need me."

Now, I do want to clarify something. When I am speaking on not being needed, I am not talking about you not having anything to offer. We have already established that you were placed in the Earth with purpose. This means that there is a need for your presence and for what God has endowed you with. We were created for two reasons: 1) to minister to the heart of God and 2) to minister to the heart of God's creation.

The word minister, by definition, is to serve. This means we have an essential responsibility to serve others. Therefore, when it comes to how you serve and why you serve, you are needed to get the job done. There is something that needs to be done to grow and move the human dynamic, and you have what is needed to assist in that effort. So, you are needed, regarding having something to offer the world, having something that the world needs. However, as it relates to forcing others to need you in order for them to function or succeed, you cannot have such a requirement. You will be disappointed almost every time. Again, there will be times that, regardless of what you bring to the table, you and your efforts will not even be recognized. People have destroyed good relationships, left jobs, relocated, changed goals, all because someone did not recognize, call upon, or praise them. You must know who you are, what you offer, and be secure in that thing whether you are noticed, are needed, or are celebrated. This is especially true since most people and places are steppingstones. Do not allow steppingstones to become mud or cement because you did not feel appreciated.

You Don't Need to be Necessary

If I were invited to the White House, and I stepped into a room full of dignitaries, it does not mean that I must lack confidence, so that I might step into that space, humbly? I understand that because of who God made me and what He placed on the inside of me that wherever I go, I add value to that space. Therefore, even in a room full of dignitaries, I matter. There is something of value that I am adding to that moment and to those individuals, just as much as there is something I am drawing out. It is with this in mind that I also recognize that, though I am of value, I am not necessary. That moment and those individuals are sufficient with or without my presence. I am just an extra dose of awesome.

Let's look at it another way. On a job, I know what I bring to the table. I understand that I am needed there and that because I operate in excellence, there is good fruit being produced based on what my presence and work adds to the tasks. However, I also understand that if I were to leave that job or get fired from that position tomorrow, the business will go on without me, and the work will still get done. I am needed to get the work done, but I am not necessary to see it brought to fruition. In Layman's terms, I am replaceable.

Here is something most of us fail to grasp. When you obligate yourself to be necessary, you stop being needed. This means you are no longer useful. It does not mean that you do not have value or resources. It means that you have made it so much about you that you have made a graven image of yourself when you were called to be a *living sacrifice*. Graven images take up space. They are good to look at, but they do not meet needs. When you make yourself necessary, you make yourself destructible. No wonder we self-sabotage so much. We want to be needed so much, that we project ourselves as necessary. Do not ever think so highly of yourself that you believe another will not be able to function without you. Reversely, do not ever think so little of yourself that you require someone to need and you, to build up confidence and security within yourself. You are replaceable, and that is okay. Knowing such should have you honor your role in another's life more.

I want to look at this from one more particularly important standpoint, from a relational standpoint, both friendly and intimate. So often, we meet people, and we insert necessity into the equation. We see that we have things in common, and it feels good, so we make those persons we connect to necessary for our well-being. In these moments, we tell ourselves that rejection is unlikely. That is dangerous because we lack preparation and healthy response to rejection when it occurs.

For example, a leader or a mentor meets a young man who appears to have great potential. That leader makes himself a necessary part of that young man's life hoping to help to grow him. That leader feels that he has some level of wisdom and experience that he can share that would help mature the young man, and so he takes on the responsibility, which later becomes ownership of that individual's growth. This is concerning because in that moment, the leader begins to view that young man as a project, a son, a brother, maybe even a friend. If the young man does not reciprocate or appreciate what the leader is trying to offer, complications arise in the relationship. And this is all because the leader made their relationship dynamic necessary. The leader's desire to be necessary jeopardized his level of effectiveness.

It could be a parent who has lost a child, an adult who wants a child but cannot have one, or a man or woman who has always wanted a sibling. He or she meets someone who seems to fit into the idea, into the fantasy of what it looks like to have one. Therefore, the man or woman not only inserts his or herself into the picture, but they also make the other individual a necessary part of his or her life as well. That creates an overwhelming burden for the recipient because that person never wanted to be put in that position. It could even be that the adult felt that the child was missing something he or she had, and so took on the responsibility of filling that void. Regardless, someone was made a necessary part of a relationship dynamic that may have not needed to have been formed.

I could address more scenarios, but I am going to end with this one that really hits home for many, as it is such a commonality in this day and age---the romantic dynamic of necessity. A man and woman meet and are attracted to each other. They make the decision to work towards getting to know each other. They talk on the phone. They go out on dates. They share likes and dislikes.

Over time, they found that the two have many things in common, and that they enjoy each other. With this discovery comes the decision to be a couple. At some point, the man and/or woman views his or her counterpart as important to his or her life and wellness. "He makes me happy.", is the justification we hear, often. It is determined that either the man has what the woman needs to function better, or the woman has what the man needs, or both.

So, where do things get messy? At the point that the companion is made vital and necessary. Quite often, in these cases, we see the two move in together. As well, they began to compromise to fulfill each other's wants and needs. For many Christians, in this case, they change standards and truths, while hoping God will still honor the relationship. So many things are done in the name of love, and it is most always because one or both persons made each other necessary to the fulfillment of the other and of self. Let me just slide this in here. You cannot break God's instruction to show love. If God is love, and He knows what it is supposed to look like, how can you dismiss God in the name of love and still think you are honoring the other individual? What you are doing is creating an idol out of that person, and that is dangerous. You cannot maintain a healthy relationship, if one or both persons are idolized.

What usually happens in a relationship when you make that person necessary for you, or you necessary for that person is compromise, self-sabotage, idolization, disappointment, disassembling of character, disloyalty, heartbreak, multiple break up-make up moments, compromise in beliefs, and the lists goes on. When you make yourself or the other an idol, nothing goes as it should, and eventually you two fall apart. Romantics, who are, innately, givers, struggle with this, greatly. They need to be needed. Romantic givers who are men have the hardest time because they enter each romantic encounter looking to be the *knight* and "Mr. Right". Thus, they give far more of themselves than they should, and far too quickly. This is even true, when it is evident that the relationship has no potential to grow, because they are hoping need trumps passion, until passion catches up. It becomes very tough when all that passion and giving is not reciprocated. Many fail to see the pattern they set, and how the dismantling of the relationship is, profusely, of their own accord.

A broken relationship, and possible friendship, is usually the result when you make your good intentions and ability to meets a person's need, a requirement for the both of you to function. You do not need to be everything to everybody. And this is with all relationship dynamics, not just romantic. So, you cannot afford to make yourself necessary, even when it comes to relationships. Say this with me, "I don't need to be necessary." You do not need to be necessary to be efficient. When you make yourself necessary, you make way for rejection, but you also give people permission to abuse you. Understand that being needed does not mean being necessary. *It does not take any value away from you if someone does not consider you necessary for his or her well-being.* This is a great truth to carry with you throughout every stage of your life.

Permit Your Difference. Embrace Your Extraordinary

It was never God's plan and design for you to be average. There is nothing wrong with being different. I believe that there is an innate piece of each person that believes this to be true. Many of us spend our entire lives trying to honor that difference and prove difference is okay. So, someone please help me out because I cannot understand, for the life of me, why we seek so hard to be something we see as so wrong. You should be proud to be one-of-a-kind. Difference is a gift to the human dynamic. **Give yourself permission to be different.** Be un-boxable and extraordinary, without apologizing for it.

We were each created uniquely. We are not supposed to look, act, sound, feel, be the same as one another. Agree with what God says about you. What's the fun in looking and living like everyone else? No fun, at all. To me, that is a miserable way to live. I await the day when being extraordinary is more of a commonality than a rarity.

In the same token, **stop apologizing when your different makes other people uncomfortable.** Their discomfort with your difference should not intimidate you. As long as you are not living in a manner that is dishonorable to both God and man, you should not allow another's disapproval to daunt you into reproaching yourself. We keep trying to avoid rejection, so we apologize for being different, in hopes that someone will accept it. We apologize through what we say and what we do. In fact, we apologize so much, that it is a natural response to anything that could make another uncomfortable. Think about how many times you say, "I'm sorry." within a week. Now, think about the situations you chose to respond with "I'm sorry." to. So many of those moments did not warrant any form of apology. We even say, "I'm sorry." in place of "Excuse me." a great deal. In apologizing for being different, we are prepping our masks, like meals for the *week*. This brings us to our next point.

Embrace the freedom to be you, unapologetically. Apologizing, or living a life that would appear to be, consistently, apologizing to others for being who God created you to be says that you are not satisfied with who He created. You are telling God that He did something wrong when He formed you, that your making was flawed. It is amazing that we seek out acceptance and validation from others because we do not believe in our own worth. I would argue that it is because we, actually, do believe we are worth something, and that causes us to seek out proof. If you do not believe you matter, nothing anyone could say about your worth will convince you of it.

So, you must believe that you are worth something to pursue validation of such. And that is the next pit we fall into. Recognizing that we are worth something, yet looking to others to determine how much, will fail us every time. You must come to that conclusion, resulting from your conversations with God, not with people. People change their minds too much, about your worth, for you to make that your source of validation.

Here is the reason why this is an issue: You are a one-of-a-kind making of the Creator, designed, carefully, within the heart, mind, and will of God. His thought shaped and molded you into the perfect specimen, filled with purpose and value. There must be something within you that can serve as a contribution to the Earth because God does not waste thought and power on what He cannot bless.

The truth of the matter is that, as the "workmanship of His hand", you are priceless; therefore, it is impossible for another to determine your worth. If you allow someone else to define your extraordinary, you are no longer extraordinary. Your authenticity and worth were determined when God thought you up. Likewise, walking in another's shadow is about your insecurities with your own footsteps. Your *different* is only wrong when it dishonors God or another. Own and celebrate the freedom you must walk in the genuineness of who God ordained you to be.

So, say this with me, with all the confidence and assurance you can muster: *"I am different, and that is okay. I am different because God made me that way. I am different, and I choose to shine. I am different. I am one-of-a-kind."* Mmm, that's good. Doesn't that feel good---to say, to believe, to know? A little quirky, I know. Still a solid truth.

Every Path Has Its Puddles

I recognize that much of what we are made to feel ashamed of is the various paths we take in life, both the things we can control and the things we cannot. Rejection plays a huge role in this, often determining how we live out truth. There is something I tell people all the time: "God cannot work with your lie." Walk out truth and love, by any means necessary.

I have a motto that I live by: *"Live. Learn. Grow."* I cannot do anything about what happened two seconds ago, whether of my own accord or not. **I lived** it. What can **I learn** from it? And how can I use the experience to **grow**? With that being said, **stop being embarrassed about your truths. Own your truths**.

The older I get, the more that instruction matters. As well, the older I get, the more its meaning grows for me. Before, it was about learning from life-----my interactions, my good decisions, my bad decisions, the consequences of both, my successes and failures, my spiritual growth, my positioning. The goal became and remains gaining wisdom regardless of the route taken. As I have gotten older and matured, "Live. Learn. Grow." looks a little different for me, or rather its meaning has additional qualities and truths.

Many, who have known me, know that I have always been a very private person. One reason for this is that there have been times when I have shared the "Me" I sleep with, and he was mishandled. Thus, I have always be cautious about who I share what with. I understand that *not everyone can handle your truths.* However, I have also learned that one must be careful not to allow caution and wisdom to become fear and intimidation. That can lead to self-entrapment. I have always been quite a fearless guy. I mean, I have had a great deal to combat over the course of my life. Yet, the times I have really struggled with fear (specifically the fear of rejection) are when it is time to be honest about my inner truths.

Over the years, I grew a fear of rejection as a response to being see-through. That fear became my defense. Part of it was because I did not want to experience rejection. Part of it was because I do not like being in the spotlight, especially for the wrong reasons. Part of it was because I did not want to prove people right, when their truths of me were so wrong...You know those "I told you so." and "I knew it." moments. This was especially true when I had lived out what they thought. Part of it was because I had received so much ridicule for what seemed like everything under the sun, that I did not want to incur more persecution and attack.

Regardless of the reason, overtime I noticed that I began to walk fearful of people's response to my story, to my truth. So, I just kept it in, and died slowly [inwardly], while looking strong outwardly. The few times I was courageous enough to share, what was shared was mishandled and abused. So, the fear of sharing, of being open and transparent, grew. It was interesting that people would praise me on my transparency, not knowing how little I was open about. My goal became to share enough to make a point---*to share without sharing,* as I call it.

Many of us do that. I am sure you do that. It is discomforting, having to hold it in. I know that I am not the only one who has ever fallen into the cycle of mistrust, fear, and discomfort. Such things effect our well-being.

From a young age, I could consider myself like David in the field, communing with God. I was used to being transparent and vulnerable with God because it seemed that it was all I had growing up. However, I struggled to open up to people. Even though I was honest, I was not always vulnerable. I settled into the honest portion of what I shared while still sharing very little. I was afraid of how my truths (the good, the bad, the ugly) would be handle because, studying people my entire life, I saw how they mishandled the vulnerability of others. I did not feel I could trust my vulnerability to anyone. Things are different now. I had to allow myself to walk through a time of vulnerability, transparency, and trust with people. So, God took me on a journey of vulnerability. I gave the "Me" I sleep with permission to step out in public, flaws and all.

During my journey of opening up to people, I realized that in an effort to hide from people, at some point, I began hiding from God also. I did not realize that I had begun to allow my secrecy and avoidance of people to become a part of my relationship with God. At some point, I just did not share much. Part of it was because I assumed since God already knew, there was no need to regurgitate. Part of it was because I hide created a habit of hiding. And, since I do things in extreme, when I hid, I hid. Little did I realize that God was a recipient. I began hiding the things I knew He could handle, and wanted to give me peace in. If I am honest, part of it was because I wanted to waddle in pity; I didn't want to be accountable to growing out of whatever pit I had settled in. Having taken this journey of vulnerability, I believe the more vulnerable I became with people, the more vulnerable I became with God (even more than I used to be), until it began to balance out.

What I discovered is that *I was asking people, who had no capacity to honor my truths, to do so. I was obligating others to perform with a grace they did not have.* I felt that, if I trusted you that much, there was no room for fallout. I was wrong because I cannot require of another that he or she act in a manner for which there is no capacity. *God is the only one who can truly handle all our truths. And though He places individuals in our lives with the grace to honor them, we still do not have a right to obligate even those individuals to guard our truths.*

Due to this experience, I have learned an especially important strategy to walking confidently and vulnerably that I want to share with you. **Be vulnerable with God, so that you can be confident with others.** As well, **do not share with another what you have not, first, shared with God.** *Anything that I am willing to share with someone else is something I have already shared with God and* *found peace in.* If God is cool with it, no matter how destructive, humiliating, shocking it may be, there is nothing another can say that will change how He feels about it. If God forgives it, you do not need someone else to forgive it. If God blesses it, you do not need someone else to bless it. This requires us to have conversations---real, soul-infused conversations with ourselves. The "Me" I sleep with and I talk daily. Truth never escapes us, no matter how piercing it may be.

When we seek out the approval of others, we are telling God that He is not enough and that we are not enough. We are telling God that the way He sees us is a mistake. We are telling a consistent, pure, honest, loving God that inconsistent, wicked, dishonest, disloyal people have a better view of our worth than He does. This is so, horribly, wrong and dysfunctional. What God has to say about it is all the answer you need.

Many think it takes courage to speak truth. I believe this is true, in some cases. I also believe that courage is not needed at the point that you own your truth. I believe courage is needed when you are devaluing or allowing others and the expectation of their response to devalue your truth. Thus, the courage needed to speak it becomes a factor. I believe that, at the point that you own your truth, and you have peace about your truth, the level of vulnerability and ease for which you can speak it does not require courage; it requires commitment. It requires follow-through. It requires impact, and a specific positioning to make sure that impact is made. I believe that when you are expressing that truth, it is effective to who you are directing it to, even if that means that the *boomerang* effect of peace, joy, release, ends up on you.

Why am I telling you all of this? Am I trying to make this all about me or just going off on a tangent? No...though I have been known to be a *soap box*er from time to time. The reason is because I have come to a place where **I give people permission not to agree with or accept my truths.** I have learned to **stop being embarrassed about my story**, and to own my truths. You, too, must come to that place. That is, if you are not there already. If you are, stay there.

We walk through life and let people determine what about our life is okay and what about our life is unacceptable. We walk through life letting people try to determine what is acceptable and what is not. This becomes a problem because *people will determine your worth based on what about your story they agree or disagree with.* Which goes back to the whole point of this conversation, insecurities. Our insecurities cause us to seek others out for our worth. Yet, the scale upon which people measure our worth is, extremely, flawed. If you are not careful, you will allow people to make you feel so small and insignificant.

Insecurity is rejection's proof that it is doing its job. Giving in often leads to rejection becoming insecurity's hope. This means, if you do not know what you bring to the table, your insecurities will invite rejection to dinner, and you are liable to miss a meal (opportunity).

So, *stop being embarrassed about your truths.* That is your story. You will live a life that will include good decisions and bad decisions. That is why God is merciful. He understands that we are not going the get it right all the time. God also understands that we are going to experience hurts and some mind-blowing, life-altering moments that make us question who we are (and who He is). As well, stop being ashamed of things that are out of your control. There are some experiences in life that you could nothing different to change the outcome. So, why walk in shame? It is very disheartening that when we are not choosing to be victim, we are choosing to live in shame. How about move victory? You survived that thing.

Now, when I say stop being embarrassed, it does not mean that you disregard how your story, the things you may have said and done, can affect another or can move your life. We, always, want to be mindful, empathetic, and considerate of the impact we have the potential to make, and that we have made. on our life or someone else's.

What I am saying is, every human on this planet will fail, at some point---numerous times to be exact. Failure is not an option; it is inevitable. Defeat is not an option; it is a choice. So, why let people's opinions and perceptions of you beat you down because you failed in their eyes?

Whatever puddle you find yourself stepping or falling in, own the experience, get cleaned up, and learn from it. But, whatever you do, do not hide from it. You do not want the puddle to become a pit.

Rejection Has a Face

The Reflection of Rejection

When you look in the mirror, what do you see? Do you see love, joy, peace, grace, hope, virtue? Or do you see hate, depression, confusion, weakness, doubt, worthlessness, rebellion? Your soul has a reflection. Just the same, rejection has its own reflection. And each time you reflect within yourself, you must be willing and able to access whether you are reflecting rejection, and if so, how much?

Rejection tells you that there is something missing, something lacking, something broken in your life, and in you. Rejection teaches you to never be content, and to always complain. Rejection encourages isolation, serving as one-on-one time with yourself, to bring up and regurgitate all that feels and looks wrong and out of place in your life. When you are walking with vision, hope, and grace, rejection brings in comparison and fear for an intervention, to ensure that you get back on track---however wrong that track may be.

You see, if I am not careful, rejection will go from guiding the "Me" I sleep with to becoming the "Me" I sleep with. And, if I am supposed to be a temple where the Holy Spirit, my spiritual, live-in maintenance man, can reside, then rejection is an unwelcomed guest, taking up too much space. And those who know me, know how I feel about my space. What I am doing, when I allow rejection occupancy within me, is making it uncomfortable for the Holy Spirit to stay. It is the same Holy Spirit that provides me with peace, joy, love, patience, endurance, and more. And the same is true for you.

Rejection will be a part of your life, but you do not have to give it a home. Guard your heart. Shield your mind. Assess your life. If you are walking in depression, self-hate, hate for others, envy, fear, doubt, rebellion, chaos and confusion, worthlessness, have a poor view of self, any of these and more, you have likely come to a place that you are gravitating to, believing, and walking out the lies that rejection keeps reflecting within you. And, if you believe them within, that reflection will extend itself into your behavior and interactions. Your entire demeanor will reflect rejection, if that is what you continue to feed on and digest.

Know this. Defeat is never an option because victory always is. The way to know victory is to be self-aware and committed to the truth of who God ordained you to be, while allowing the Holy Spirit to help you walk in the grace---strength, courage, and wisdom----God has endowed you with. Do not settle for a reflection that is corrupted and despicable. *Because **what you reflect, inwardly, you will project outwardly.*** *It is important to understand that whether rejection is experienced or perceived, everything you do from the point of feeling it, is on you.* You cannot help that you feel. None of us can control our emotions. However, you are responsible for how you respond to what you feel. It is very dangerous for you to live from the posture of your insecurities because it causes you to be imbalanced spiritually, mentally, emotionally, and physically. As well, doing so puts you at risk of being a repeat offender. By this, I mean that you risk assaulting others with your emotions. Consider how many people, and even things, in life that you have, emotionally, battered because you did not know how to handle rejection, or you allowed your insecurities to get the best of you. The reflection of rejection can lead to physical and verbal abuse on self and others. That is why it is extremely important that you learn yourself. You would be amazed at how many people you can just see "Insecurity" written all over. And their actions only serve to validate that they feel they have something to prove and something to earn. The unnecessary tearing down of others is one major sign that a person is not secure within his or her self. Consider yourself like a clock. You must learn how you tick. It is sad that most take time to know others far more than they do themselves. You should know the mechanics of your own soul much more than you do another. Learn the stance of your soul, so that you can be aware of what it reflects in your life.

When the Man in the Mirror Doesn't Love Me

There's this song by Gospel singer, Marvin Sapp titled, "The Best In Me". It came out years ago, and though the chorus was simple, man did it stir up the masses. We had already been in this phase of the *haters* and *fake friends*, and all that. So, when this song came out, you would think that no one thought well of another because so many sung the lyrics with such aggression and passion. The chorus simply says, "He saw the best in me, when everyone else around me could only see the worst in me." For many they took these lyrics as a way to lash back at those who tried to hold them accountable to having integrity and being the best version of themselves. For some, this song was their message to the *haters*. For others, they followed through with the purpose of the song, and were empowered.

This is a good song with a good message. I wish more took the song for what it was rather than what they wanted it to be. Why did I mention this song and its lyrics? That's simple. Each time I heard the song on the radio or at church, I could not help but think of how easy it was to leave ourselves out of the underlining truth of that message. I have learned that, eventually, it is not about what everyone else sees or believes; at some point, we are the enemy disguised as the victim. We often see the worst in ourselves, with no help from anyone else.

I often tell people when talking about rejection or ungratefulness or disappointment---things along those lines---that *no one needs help being negative.* If I were to ask you, right now, to get a sheet of paper and write all the things that you do not like about yourself or your life, it would take much more time for you to write than it would for you to think. In fact, not only would you be able to express your issues with ease, but I also have no doubt that you would need more than one sheet of loose leaf or legal paper to get the job done. Now, if I asked you to write down all the things you like about yourself or your life, not only would you pause for a moment and have to really think, but I would not be shocked if you barely filled the front side of one page. This, again, is because no one needs help being negative. We must, however, work at being or remaining positive.

We sit in front of the mirror, we lay on our beds, we even drive and daydream, thinking about what's wrong with us, what we did wrong, what we could fail at next, what we should not try (for fear of failure), who we should not interact with (for fear of rejection), what the future holds, if anything at all, and the list goes on and on. So, we look in the mirror, and lament over a man or woman that does not really have to exist. It's the rejection talking. The masks we wear, daily, might give us a positive outward appearance, but even our shadow reflects our inner truths.

What I know is that no one knows the "Me" I sleep with. And no matter how much of him that I reveal to the world, there is a portion of him that remains hidden and broken.   That guy is the version of me that self-hates and even loathes me. That guy is the version of me that creates, what seems like, a never-ending echo of "You'll never fit in." or "You'll always be a failure." or "They'll never like you, so don't waste your time." or even "You know, they were right about you." There is a piece of each us that we hide from the world.

How sad is it that, when you look in the mirror, you settle for guilt, low-esteem, denial, doubt, fear, anger, abandonment, neglect, rejection, when you could gravitate to truth instead? I mourn individuals who walk in shame of what they have said and done. I have been one of those individuals. Know that there is freedom and peace made readily available for you to live outside of that guilt and shame. I weep for individuals who deny themselves the very essence of their beings, so that they might fit the status quo and avoid rejection. I am saddened by those who stride, discouraged and fearful. I am concerned for those who are always bitter and resentful, angry, and discontent. I grieve for the individuals who choose to be a victim because it is easy and comfortable to shift blame rather than take responsibility. It breaks my heart to see those who are willing to settle for being less than their best because they do not want the responsibility that accompanies greatness.

And so, when the "Me" I sleep with seeks out opportunity to exhort himself to walk in those things, I must remind him of what I know to be true about who he is. You must do the same. Every time, rejection and its little friends creep up to tell you the lies about your existence, you respond with "I am who God says that I am." "I can do what God says that I can do." "I will be who God says that I will be." You can follow it with some inward accountability. "I am my worst enemy. My only roadblock is me." You make those confessions. Have a conversation with your roadblocks. Set the record straight. Do not get stuck because you refuse to be honest.

When the man in the mirror does not love me, that is an opportunity for me to evaluate my version of truth, and readjust, not the reflection, but the being. So often, we work at changing the reflection, while we leave the being dysfunctional. We produce from the very essence of who we are. I must assess my inner fruit and evaluate what type of tree or garden I am growing. If, when I look in the mirror, I cannot see love all over me, I have accepted that lie rejection has introduced to me that I do not matter. I am choosing to believe that I am an accident, I am not loved, I am my past, and I am my failures. When you give in to these lies, you are corrupting your reflection.

There are plenty of others ready and willing to call you a failure, a fool, a loser, a nobody, a waste of thought, a waste of time, a waste of good air and space; do not you ever say it of yourself. We must get to a place of being at peace with our reflection. The only way that will happen is when the man or woman in the mirror is solidified in the reality of whom he or she is, based on the truth of God's design and call for him or her. Simply put, **you must make God's truth your reality.**

Perspective is Everything

Now, this may make me feel old, and you older, but when I was a kid, I used to hear statements like "Your word is everything.", "My word is bond.", or various things along those lines. A person was expected to produce actions that would fulfill or validate what he or she spoke. We were taught that your actions are proof that you mean what you say. I also grew up hearing about the way one is to carry his or herself in public because 1) you were representing your parents, and 2) people will judge you based on how you act, or how they perceive your actions. In fact, we were taught that people perceive you based on how you carry yourself, not who you are. The only time we seemed to hear about the way we thought, was regarding education and career choices. Therefore, we were, subconsciously, conditioned to believe that our mind was a worker-bee and how we thought was work----that thinking was a job that was associated with living.

Sadly, the biggest thing we were taught to think about was not, what information we could gather from reading or school lessons; it was not even about what our future careers would be. The biggest thought any human has even been taught to entertain is "Do they like me?". In addition, we were taught to keep at the forefront of our minds, questions like "What do they think about me?", "Why can't I be like them?", "Am I better than they are?", and many more insecurity-based questions. We were taught to think comparison, look for acceptance, and to be fearful of rejection. Like Legion, each day of our lives, we put on multiple masks (personalities), and with each mask comes a different behavior, a different vernacular, a different disposition, and a different perspective. The crazy thing about it is that these masks do not make us different; they make us common. And, we have way too many copies. We refuse to live "outside of the box" because we refuse to think outside of it. We treat being extraordinary like it is a sin. We act like cell phones or cars. Each year, just being an updated version of the same type. If this is you, **stop settling for being an updated version of the outdated clone to an original masterpiece.** You are an original masterpiece. There is no need to settle for being the clone to another.

Who told us it was okay to live life on the assembly line? Again, we have way too many copies because we are afraid people will reject our "organic". If we produce from the essence of who we are, where is the authentic production of that essence?

Now, I believe that we all begin as thinkers and that as we are taught to change behavior and speech, the way we think changes. Some may disagree when they consider education. Think about it though. You are told you should not **act** like that or **say** that, not you should not **think** like that. It is not until we grow older that we are then asked to consider how we think and how it affects what we say and do. That is why we have such a fight when we get older.

When you grow up changing behavior to change perspective, it becomes quite difficult to switch gears at the point of "adulting". When you are taught that behavior develops character rather than that one's perspective does, it is a huge eye-opener when you realize that is not the case. If you are taught, as a child, that your behavior makes you, how shocking and somewhat unfair is it to then be required to revamp and move towards perspective? It is one's perspective that truly drives and defines image.

We allow rejection to cause us to create unhealthy perspectives for ourselves, and then we live life through those lenses. Perspective is everything. How you view things will determine how you move through life. "What you see is what you get." used to be a popular saying. I believe it is also true that what you see is what you give. You share with the world the version of you that you see in the mirror. When you agree with rejection's proclamation and begin to see hate, fear, regret and shame, hopelessness and depression, failure, unforgiveness, loneliness, abuse, pain, worthlessness, etc., that is exactly what you will share with the world. What you reflect inwardly will reflect outwardly. Remember we produce from who we are.

There is a song by Bishop Paul S. Morton & the FGBFC Mass Choir (lead vocalist is Pastor William Murphy). The song is entitled, "I Am What You See." The lyrics are:

"Help me to see me the way that You see me.

At times, I see pain, Lord, when You see victory.

I see where I am. You see where I shall be.

Open my eyes. Help me believe, I am what You see."

What a beautiful prayer. So, often we run to God with all these needs and wants, never really asking God to help us see ourselves the way He sees us. There are those who do go to God with that prayer, but either never wait for the answer, or they allow what people and circumstances have to say to supersede what God has spoken. Do not waste of a prayer, if you're going to do that.

When you can view yourself through the lens of Heaven, you then know how to respond when you encounter things and people who work to contradict it. Never ever view anything through lens of rejection, whether it is self-inflicted, perceived, or experienced. Create and establish your point of reference from a place of truth and love. India Arie's song, "I Am Light" is a perfect example of what that looks like. In fact, her first song "Video" is also a great example. Side note: *I believe "I Am Light" is a matured version of "Video", both having the same concept of self-awareness and security.* Creating the proper perspective has everything to do with allowing God to be your leader, life to be your teacher, rejection to be a feature, and hope to be your friend.

The Confession of Rejection

Take a moment to exhale and inhale. As you exhale, release all the things that deprive you of life. As you inhale, take in all the things that revive and empower your life.

You are what you see, and you are what you say. Quite often, we outtalk truth and wellness, both intentionally and blindly. There are certain things people do not have permission to call me. Just the same, I am mindful of what I pronounce over myself, as well as what I answer to. Our words have power, so much power, that whatever I speak requires, of itself, circulation in my life to the point of manifestation. That is why you cannot lose hope when you keep declaring things you are not seeing. Eventually, they will show up. That is also why we cannot allow rejection to produce unhealthy confessions.

"I am a failure." is not something that you should allow to part from your lips. "Nobody loves me." is also not something that you should utter. "I guess it's going to always be like this." is another falsity you should not declare over your life. See, the big problem is that everything you speak, with rejection and comparison as your point of reference, is a lie. You cannot expect truth to reign in your life when you keep releasing lies with your tongue. What you say matters. Properly govern your confessions for yourself, for your life, and for others. Be a good steward over your vernacular because your language is authoritative.

I have a saying, which I derived from the scripture, Ephesians 4:29. The saying is "If it does not edify, it should not be verbalized." This simply means that if your words do not build and uplift, speak them not. Do not release them into the atmosphere; keep them out of your world and anyone else's. Rejection has its own confession. It does not have to become yours. Combat rejection's declarations with truth. "Speak only what elevates and not what depreciates", also derived from Ephesians 4:29. "Easier said than done", you might say. It is okay. Work at it. You will get it. Be intentional. Be self-aware. Be accountable. And be honest.

Dear God

One of the biggest questions a person will ever asked is "God, what is the story You wrote about me?" The answer to that question will be your sustaining grace. *Once you know the story, or at least have a glimpse of the story God wrote about you when He placed you in the Earth, you will no longer give people the power to measure your worth or dictate how you live.* **Accept that you are flawed and be honest about what those flaws are. Stop allowing people to imprison you to a flawless life.** That is an obligation that no one should be burdened with. It is impossible to live flawless. So, *stop giving people so much authority over the way you view your flaws.*

Give yourself permission to fail even your own expectations. It does not matter whether others are okay with it or not. Just like you must give people permission to fail you, you must give yourself permission to fail. When you do so, you remove the pressure to meet others' expectations. You also free yourself from the pressure of creating expectations you have little to no capacity to meet. You remove the power of another to

devalue you. As well, you decide not to devalue yourself.
That decision to free yourself, however, is on you.

In Matthew 25, there is a parable of a farmer who gave
three servants talents or units. Each man received a
different amount. One man received 5 units of shekel.
One received 2 units of shekel. The last received 1 unit
of shekel. The first two men took their shekels and
increased them. The man with the one talent buried his
talent and left it buried.

When each man was confronted about what he did with
the talents received, the first two men had something to
show for it, but the final servant made excuses and
justified lack of fruit. The excuse he gave was that he was
not given enough to work with. This was simply because
he received less than the others. Comparison will get you
every time. There are many points in this account. One
important point is that the man with one talent failed to
realize what he had was enough. Instead of taking what
he was given and using it to grow more, he dismissed its
value and tucked it away.

Yes, you will experience rejection, and you should grow
to be okay with that. You should not spend your days
comparing yourself to anyone else. *Whenever we utilize,*

or in my opinion, use up our thought, energy, and air to take time and compare ourselves and our lives to another, we are, in that moment, telling the very Air we breathe (God, Himself) that He has wasted His breath on us, and that the story He wrote about us is a lie. What you are telling God is that your *different* is not good enough, that your different is a flaw in design. This is often the result of comparing ourselves, and what we have, to others. We neglect to celebrate what we have on the inside of us and see it as enough. Hear me clearly, when I say this: **What you have is enough because who you are is enough.** Your fruit is based on your worth. You must, first, recognize your worth or you will get nowhere.

You are enough based on the story that God wrote about you when He thought you into existence. Do not exhaust another breath believing and embracing the lie, rejection serves, that declares otherwise.

Ultimately, what God says about you is what matters most. What God says about you is what you should be basing your worth, your purpose, your success, your influence on. We can say so many things about seeking the approval of others and being okay with rejection.

There are other books out about it. There have been sermons and conversations about it. No matter what else can be said, the truth of the matter is that our identity is solidified by our Creator.

What God says about you is what matters. If you do not know what God thinks about you, you will always be at risk of "approval addiction". You will always be seeking out validation from people. I do not care how confident you say you are, or how well you say you know yourself, if you have not discovered "you" from God's point of view, you are missing some of identity and security. So, the key is growing close to God. Build an intimate relationship with God and allow Him to teach you what you are supposed to look and walk like in the Earth. You are made in His likeness and image. So, the more you discover about God, the more you discover about yourself.

And, as you make new discoveries, embrace them. You cannot expect others to embrace a truth about who you are that you choose to reject. So, I know we asked this question earlier, but let us do it, together, once more. "Dear God, what is the story you wrote about me?" Keep seeking the answer to that question. As you receive the answer, do not bury it or throw it away, like the man with the one talent. Hide it in your heart and mind. Seek God for the grace to live it out. Allow it to grow and increase within you.

Acceptance is a Bonus

Now, really this whole thing can be summed up in this next sentence. But where would the fun in that be? Pay awfully close attention to the next statement...and inhale it. **Give people permission to reject you.—*Acceptance is a bonus.*** If you give a person permission to reject you, when he or she does, it will not be such a shocker. We struggle so much because when we set expectations regarding our interactions with others, we leave little to no room for rejection; it is not written in our plans. When it happens, we do not know how to respond because we never prepared for it.

Now, I am not saying to expect rejection. To expect it is to walk in fear and timidity; that within itself is insecurity. I am saying be prepared for the possibility of being rejected, or simply misunderstood. Now, sometimes, we misplace being misunderstood with rejection. This is dangerous because doing so can lead one to adopting a "victim" mentality. For many, with such a mentality, their point of reference is rooted in being misunderstood.

Rejection, neglect, abandonment, are just a few of the feelings that accompany this victimized view on self, and it trickles over into numerous areas of a person's life. For example, a person does not agree with something you said, or has a different point of view. Now you are a "victim", misunderstood and rejected. It was your ideas that were rejected, not you. Isn't it amazing how personal we make the things that are not real personal? Someone rejects something you do; therefore, he or she is rejecting you. That is such a horrible way to look at life; yet it is how most people perceive things. This foolish notion that, if someone accepts what you say or do, that person accepts you, or if someone rejects what you say or do, he or she rejects you, must come to an end.

We define ourselves by what we say or do, not by who we are. We do not understand that *what we say and do is the fruit of who are, not the foundation.* Such a wrong viewpoint teaches us to be performance-driven. We try to perform our way into acceptance, into success, into love, into joy, into peace, into greatness, and the list goes on.

The truth of the matter is that you are rejectable. Yes, you have much to offer the world, and you are a gift. However, no one, I repeat, no one is obligated to receive and embrace you. That is a personal right; that is not a human right. It cannot be the requirement of another.

The sooner that you are willing to accept that you are rejectable, and people have the right to reject you, the more secure and effective you will be. I say this because we have grown the habit of setting expectations based on the rejection we experience or perceive in our lives. We require people to accept us and throw tantrums when they do not.   I am going to say it the way I feel it----Get over yourself. Stop making everything about you. Acceptance is a bonus.

Motivational speaker, Lisa Nichols, made a statement during an interview that is exactly how I view things. I have been told that I am mean and arrogant for this view. So, Lisa, I guess we are both mean and arrogant (LOL). The statement was this: *"See, we want to grow, but we want to stay liked by everybody. I was willing to be my own rescue at the risk of your approval."* She went on to say my favorite part, which is, *"We want to be liked. Well, I woke up and I liked myself today. So, your "like" is extra. My job is to like me first."* She continued with her willingness to ask herself *"Lisa, do you like you? Lisa, are you proud of you?",* and she was willing to do it every day, *"before I checked in with anyone else.",* she stated.

Now, that right there. That is so important because we are constantly checking in with other people to validate the worth of our being and of our day. Think about it. How many mornings do you start your day, not by thanking God for a new morning, or by affirming yourself, but by checking your Facebook, Instagram, Snapchat, Twitter, and other social media accounts to see, not just what is going on, but how many "likes" and "loves", how many comments and shares you received for your posts since the last time you scrolled? C'mon now. There must be a better way of going about seeking the approval and validation of others. Oh, wait! There is---- Don't. Stop seeking. It is exhausting. You will have it when you need it, and you must be okay when you do not receive it.

Step away from the greatest addiction this world has ever known---seeking the approval of people who do not have the capacity to meet your needs and love you without condition. Because that is the issue. Acceptance from man is conditional. The existence of rejection is proof of that. There will always be a condition you do not meet; therefore, acceptance is never guaranteed. Approve of yourself, regardless of whether anyone else does or not.

Conclusion

One thing I have learned, and know to be true, after all these years, is that regardless of what someone says or what circumstances you have in your life, as you grow older, there is nothing or no one that can keep you from being who God called you to be, but you. There is not one bit of rejection you can experience that can launch you outside of the will of God, except you empower it to. Every single experience, good or bad, moves you towards your destiny. Therefore, we cannot afford to be emotionally driven. We can tamper with great vision or create harmful visions for ourselves if we are.

Every single person that has ever spoken ill of me or bullied me, every single bit of abuse I have received, in any form, every single situation in life that has ever disappointed me or brought me harm, every single circumstance, every high, every low, all the good and all the not-so-favorable, all of it has worked to move me farther in life. All of it has equipped me. All of it has taught me. All of it has served to motivate me. All of it has become my momentum. All of it has challenged and inspired, nurtured, and cultivated me.

I had no clue how much rejection had to do with the man I would become, until I became him. And then, I got to look back and see that regardless of what it (rejection) has had to say about my life, what God has spoken, let no man and no thing put to rest. I have learned to welcome rejection. I thought, for so long, that rejection was the worst thing that could happen to me, and many of us are taught the same thing. Truth of the matter is that rejection is a friend. It can grow us if we let it. Rejection does not have to defeat us.

I no longer live fear of rejection, in any form that it presents itself. I recognize its place and purpose in my life. I have grown to appreciate it. Though I do not have to agree with what it says, I am responsible for recognizing when it decides to rear its ugly head in my life. Then, I can also decide how to utilize it for my benefit. I understand, more than ever, that rejection can either grow me or defeat me. The choice is, ultimately, mines.

I, also, understand that, sometimes, rejection is necessary to position us where we need to be (even if it's not where we want to be). Not every situation deserves a "Yes." Remember, positioning is everything. Consider that when making career moves, building relationship, or trying to advance in life in other ways. Sometimes, rejection serves to move us in the right direction, whether we can see it or not.

Yes, I could have spoken on rejection on a deeper, more intimate level. I could have even covered numerous scenarios in which rejection plays juggler to our souls. However, the purpose of this book is simply to promote an intimate conversation about rejection and its effect on our existence. I also wanted to kill the myth that rejection is something to be conquered. As you have read, I hope you have concluded that rejection is something to embrace.

Now, you may have noticed that I repeated several statements on numerous occasions, throughout your reading. That was intentional, I assure you. It was not because I was running out of things to say. Those words are important. So important, that I encourage you to get a highlighter, and go back over the text. Each time you see a statement repeated, highlight it. You are welcomed to even highlight statements you found valuable that might have not been reiterated. Revisit those words from time to time, and recite them out loud, on occasion.

I pray that you received a few tools that will help you embrace rejection without empowering it or using it as a crutch. I, personally, look forward to being able to have this conversation with more people. Mrs. Priscilla Shirer, I would love to be a guest on *The Chat*, to discuss this topic and more.

So, let's end this the way we began. Are you ready? Say this with me (and this time I want you to insert your name each time: "[Insert name] is loved, accepted, and needed." "[Insert name] was designed on purpose, with purpose." "[Insert name]'s existence is not an accident. [Insert name] is supposed to be here. And I, [Insert name] have something to offer." God bless you.

Songs
of
Affirmation

I would be remised if I did not leave you with a list of songs that I believe relate to the topic of our conversation, songs that will serve to empower you. Some of these are prayers. Some of these may challenge you. But I pray that all of them will inspire you. I know that there are other great songs (old and new) in existence; so, feel free to add to the list, as desired. Listen and enjoy.

<u>Artist</u>	<u>Song</u>
Jonathan McReynolds	*Comparison Kills*
	Pressure
	Lovin' Me
	Smile
	Cycles
India Arie	*Healing*
	A Beautiful Day
	I Am Light
	Video
	Just Do You
	Little Things
	Get It Together
	Private Party
	Soulbird Rise
	Break the Shell

Casey J	*Journal*
Dayanna Redic	*I'm Not What You See*
Christina Aguilera	*Beautiful*
Bishop Paul S. Morton	*I Am What You See*
Kirk Franklin	*Imagine Me*
	Hello Fear
	Chains
Jill Scott	*Golden*
Joshua Micah	*Who Says?*
Musiq Soulchild	*Alive and Well*
Donald Lawrence	*Happy Being Me*
Pharrell Williams	*Happy*
Michael Buble'	*Feeling Good*
Kim Burrell	*Don't Count Me Out*
Jessica Hitte	*You Notice Me*
Resound	*Keep On Lovin'*
Dante Bowe	*Potter and Friend*
Kelly Price	*Just As I Am*
Anthony Evans	*Fighting for Me*
Smokie Norful	*Where Would I Be?*
Steffany Gretzinger	*Out of Hiding*
James Arthur	*Remember Who I Was*
Lauryn Hill	*The Miseducation of Lauryn Hill*

Different

I am different, and that is okay.

I am different because God made me that way.

I am different, and I choose to shine.

I am different. I am one-of-a-kind.

Unapologetically, from the inside, out.

I'm extraordinary, no doubt.

I am different. Look how I shine...

Bright like a diamond in a coal mine.

My different is love.

My different is hope.

My different is joy.

My different is dope.

My different is a gift that can change the world.

My different is priceless.

My different is awesome.

My different is extraordinary.

It cannot be measured. It cannot be defined....

Not by the clothes I wear, or the car I drive.

Not by where I live, or the number of 0's behind the dollar sign.

I am unique in every way.

It's because I was created that way.

And if extraordinary had a name,

my different would be its face.

www.ingramcontent.com/pod-product-compliance
Lightning Source LLC
Chambersburg PA
CBHW070717250726
48662CB00001B/467